A word from the Author

Talking to people is hard. It doesn't matter if you're going on a blind date or trying to land a job interview, speaking with someone new for the first time can be daunting. But no matter how nervous you might be, the only way to overcome this feeling is practice. Which is where books like this come in. This book will teach you all about avoiding common rejection triggers, speaking your mind confidently and articulately, and making a lasting first impression. It's a must-read for anyone who wants to feel more confident in themselves and their conversations with others.

I hadn't noticed how much we crave talking to others, even strangers, before the COVID pandemic hit us. I got bored working from home and would occasionally visit nearby coffee shops and restaurants. I realized that I was making these pitstops more and more often, even when I didn't need a drink or any food. People watching was a new hobby for me. I watched families, friends, couples, and strangers interact with each other.

People would often strike up conversations with each other or with me. I didn't think very much about it at first. I thought they were just friendly. I started to notice a pattern in how they all started a conversation. As I always had my laptop with me and something visual on the screen (my work), they would inquire about it. It was always one of three questions:

- Your work looks interesting (I work in advertising)?

- How's the coffee here?

- Are you working from home today?

Do you think any of these people really cared whether I was working from home or not? Or whether my work was of real interest to them? Of course not. They were looking for someone to chat with and asking an "innocent" question seemed like a good way to start a conversation.

There's a way to start conversations with people you don't know. Pick up artists call it cold approaching; marketers call it networking.

I'm writing this book to outline the strategy I've developed and to share with you what I've learned after years of practice. It's possible that you've had a similar experience as me, or you could be the most socially inept person in the world. My goal is to take your current situation and teach you how to break the ice with anyone.

I'll give you strategies for breaking the ice that I've found to be effective in getting conversations started, and tactics for when things don't go as well as expected. I'll also show you what's going on in people's heads when they are talking to others and how it's different from what most people think.

It's possible that this book will feel like it was written just for you. I have assumed that you have no knowledge of overt body language, psychology, or social psychology before reading it. Are you ready to start?

Nijel James

About the Author

Nijel James is a writer originally from the United Kingdom, but now lives in Asia. He's studied psychology and marketing and has been applying what he's learned to social interactions for years. He's worked for start-ups in the online dating industry, where he saw just how much a common knowledge of human psychology can help people succeed with both men and women. During his spare time, Nijel writes articles about psychology and self-improvement and his previous book on productivity, 'My Excuses are Killing Me', was hugely successful, teaching the readers how to increase their productivity and also the benefits that can have on oneself.

Writing this book was one of the most rewarding experiences Nijel has ever had. As he wrote the book, he also learned so much more about social interactions than he could have alone. He hopes that this book will help other people learn just as much as it helped him while writing it.

How to use this book

This is a guide. The techniques in this book have worked for me and many of my friends. I've used some of these techniques to break the ice with complete strangers, talk to celebrities and connect with others to close a deal. This book is a toolkit to help you talk to people. You don't have to read it cover to cover. Instead, use it as a handy reference book, or as a reference when you're not sure what to say and need a few ideas.

There is never any one right way to talk to people, but there are a thousand wrong ones. The techniques in this book should give you some pointers on how to break the ice with someone. Knowledge is only entertainment until applied. Try it out and let me know how you go.

This book is full of techniques that I have used to break the ice with people. I have tested them all out, and most of them work really well. Some of my techniques are subtle, while others are more direct; some are fast acting, while others take a while to take effect – but they all have one thing in common: these techniques all deal with the same underlying principle: to show someone that you genuinely like them as a person, because if they like you as a person then they'll like hanging out with you.

Who is this book for?

1. Introverts

This book is for people who want to improve the way they interact with others. This book is for those who want to get out of their comfort zones and talk to people. Maybe you don't talk very much to the people around you, and you feel like that's a problem. Maybe you tend to get nervous and bored when talking to new people, or don't know what to talk about when doing so. This book is for people who want to learn how to talk in a way that puts others at ease and makes them feel comfortable. If you are an introvert or an extrovert, this book can help you.

2. Those seeking mates

If you are looking for a partner, this book is for you. It's about communication, but also about understanding people's motives behind their actions. No matter what your goals may be: finding a date, introducing yourself to someone you think is attractive or seeking friendship from another person, the techniques in this book will help you improve your interactions with others.

3. Corporates

In meetings, conferences, and networking events, you'll often see people asking each other leading questions. They are trying to create rapport or get a rise out of the person they're talking to. Breaking the ice can be a powerful sales or leadership tool and can be used to build trust in negotiation.

4. Salespeople

This book is for everyone who sells. Whether you sell doors, windows, musical instruments or insurance policies, there is a way to establish rapport with your customers, which will increase your chances of getting sales. This book teaches you how to do that by lowering the customer's guard and creating friendly conversations.

5. Parents and teachers

Learning how to communicate with others effectively is essential not only for those who want to socialize more but also for children who have trouble making friends or for those who have been bullied.

6. Those in a new stage of life

Meeting in-laws, starting college, first day at the workplace, meeting a new and scary boss, moving house, or taking the stage at a conference, every change in life can be daunting. Learning to communicate effectively can be a big help. Learning how to communicate will not only let you get to know others better but also help you choose the right words when it matters most.

Contents

A word from the Author

About the Author

How to use this book

Who is this book for?

Introduction

CHAPTER 1: THE BIG DEAL IN SMALL TALK

    Why do some people have so many friends?

    Why is small talk so hard?

    The key to making small talk

CHAPTER 2: A MEANINGFUL CONVERSATION

    Going big on the small talk

    Transitioning from small talk

    Remembering names

    Reading emotion through facial expressions

    Sending the right message

CHAPTER 3: WIT AND CHARM

    Listening

    Asking the good questions

    Adding in your experiences

    Developing genuine curiosity

    Recognizing conversational styles

    Matching their style

    Somewhat vulnerable

    Chapter conclusion: An exercise on rambling

    Key takeaway

CHAPTER 4: THE ARE METHOD

    The anchor

    The Reveal

    The Encouragement

CHAPTER 5: WHAT IF?

    The conversation keeps stalling

    How do I transition to another subject after exhausting the current topic?

    How do I end a conversation when the person won't stop talking?

Conclusion

Introduction

Why small talk? Breaking the ice isn't just to make friends. It's a competitive world where charming someone can give you a competitive advantage. Whether you are trying to get a promotion, looking for your next job or simply trying to start a conversation with someone new, you've certainly realized that being able to spark a conversation with anyone is essential for success. This can be daunting for most people and why people of all ages struggle to begin or maintain a conversation.

Technically, small talk is a brief exchange of remarks on superficial matters. All those mundane conversations that you have at the subway, at the grocery store, or waiting in line at the bank, but did you know that small talk is just as important at parties, professional gatherings and even when meeting someone for the first time. We've all been there where we're standing next to someone and we catch ourselves thinking of what can be said to them, which makes it seem like we don't have anything to discuss.

Small talk is used to build comfort with another person and can be used as a segue into deeper discussions. In a business setting, small talk can be used to put other people at ease and connect with them. In this way that, it's possible to get people talking and you might actually end up doing business with them.

If you're not sure what to say in a conversation or you struggle to come up with something witty every time, then you need to be more attentive. Focus on what the other person is saying instead of thinking of what you'll say next.

Small talk conversations shouldn't be stressful after all they don't have to be long or complicated but merely stimulating enough so that the other person doesn't feel uncomfortable. The most important thing is that it should be simple and easy enough for you to use at any moment during each situation.

Chapter 1: The Big Deal in Small Talk

How are the elderly able to converse with everyone? Is it because they have vast experiences and can relate things to others? Not really. It's because they were once young, they have gone through the same experiences as everyone else and have learned the value of small talk. They did not make a big deal out of it. To them, it's normal conversation that doesn't need to be forced but is just a part of life.

In this chapter, we'll look at what small talk is, why we need it and how to make it count for you. You will also learn about some great small talk tips that will get you thinking about talking in a different way as well as get you started in improving your social skills. But before we get to that, being poor in small talk goes hand in hand with being poor socially. If you are unable to converse with others, you will have difficulty in making friends and getting into relationships. The beauty of it is that it can be learnt. How do you know that it's time to go out more, to meet people and get out of your comfort zone? You are in a rut, you have been to the same places, done the same things, talked to the same people and when it comes to conversations, you haven't had any meaningful ones. It's an internal struggle as well as an emotional one.

Why do some people have so many friends?

I'm sure you know of that one guy or girl who knew everyone and always seemed to have an overflowing social calendar. He seems to make friends easily, meeting new people, talking to old ones, and never getting stuck in a rut. There are others who often end up losing touch with friends and gaining even fewer than they started with. The question is why? It's because they never had the social skills needed to build friendships or make new acquaintances?

It goes far beyond that though. It's much more than just superficial skills; it's about being able to converse in a way that isn't overly focused on superficial things but engages a conversation and keeps it interesting. Let's look at the qualities that people who can talk to anyone have and what they do to be able to do so.

1) They're curious about other people

Each one of us has a story. When you're genuinely interested in hearing another person's story, you're able to learn and relate to that person in a much deeper way. You build a relationship where both of you can be curious about each other and build the belief that everyone's interesting. People who know how to make friends aren't just more interested in other people, but it also allows them to better understand what others are interested in at the same time. They have the ability to take into consideration what others are interested in, as well as what they don't care about and why.

Empathy is a skill that's often overlooked by many. Empathy allows you to see what another person is passionate about and find the common ground between you. Allowing you to focus on the similarities that bring you together, rather than fixate on your differences.

People who are able to talk to anyone have a strong awareness of the social circles they're in and the people who occupy it. They're aware of what's going on in those circles, why people are friends and how to relate with them while bringing a different angle than most would think of. They don't just understand others, they can also understand themselves as well as their emotions.

2) They ask questions

People who have a way with conversation understand that when you ask good questions, you're able to draw someone out completely different from their normal self. Open ended questions allow you to get insight into the other person's life without forcing them to share their entire story or leaving much unsaid. The ease of closing one questions leads most people to forget about the rest of them. The ideal outcome is whenever you ask someone a question, your question results in an answer that further opens up new possibilities.

The ability to ask questions is also related to being curious and interested in other people. Open ended questions are a great way to connect with others and learn more about them from their reactions. Most people would rather answer short, simple, direct questions because those don't require much thought or contemplation before answering. It's like a reflex, they speak, and you listen. This doesn't accomplish much in terms of building a relationship but asking deeper questions will help you come to learn more about the person in front of you.

When asking questions, it's important to not only ask about their day but for opinions and thoughts as well. Asking how someone felt about something is a great way to see another side of them that makes them look at things from a different perspective. If you want to know what people are thinking, ask them directly. Anyone who dreams big wants to hear from others that they can make those dreams come true too.

3) They know how to listen

The ability to listen is often overlooked in the social skill world, but you can't have a conversation without listening. While being knowledgeable about what other people say is important, it's also important to be able to absorb what they're saying. Being able to hear someone out and understand their exact meaning before jumping into a conversation of your own allows you to get the most out of their words and show that you're listening on an emotional level. You can learn so much more when someone is willing to do the same.

Being able to listen is also related - albeit thematically - with being curious and empathetic. This goes back to the last point, being able to understand others means that you can also begin to understand yourself. Being able to get into someone's head and grasp what they're saying is important because it allows you to listen on an emotional level and relate. You don't have to go deep with a person, but you can at least give them empathy when they listen intently.

4) They know how to build rapport

Rapport is an important part of any relationship. It's what creates the foundations that helps to elevate your friendship level. Rapport happens when you're able to learn things about another person, relate and like them at the same time. Building rapport is not something that happens overnight, but you can certainly speed it up if you learn the right way to get someone close to you.

If you want a quality friendship with someone, it's going to take more than knowing everything about them. It requires curiosity in their story but also wanting to deepen the connection between them and yourself. The ability to build rapport isn't just limited to one friend though; relationships are built upon other relationships.

5) They're active listeners

A lot of people spend a lot of time figuring out what they want to say before they say it. This is a bad habit because it doesn't allow you to fully listen to the other person and may even cause you to forget what you wanted to say when the time comes. Talking about yourself is important but more important is the other person being able to talk about themselves and what they want to say. You have control over your own time, but if you're talking with others who aren't taking responsibility for their own words then they'll take up your time without getting much out of it.

Active listening is an important steppingstone in a skilled conversation. It allows both you and the person you're conversing with to get their point across. You don't have to agree but it's important to listen instead of thinking about what you're going to say next. This is the easiest way to learn from others without scaring them away with taking up too much of your time.

Why is small talk so hard?

Why do introverts dread making small talk? We could say that it drains us of our energy, we're socially anxious and all of these other reasons. However, the real reason why small talk is so hard for us is because we view the world differently. We subconsciously assume that no one is interested in the "meaningless" social chit chat that we deem a waste of our time. However, the truth is that many people like talking about useless/meaningless things. In fact, a common question that most people ask when they meet someone for the first time is "do you have any hobbies?". It's quite telling of our society in which we use small talk as an icebreaker.

We think that if we do not have anything interesting to say then there's no reason to say anything at all. It may seem like no one cares what we have to say but you're wrong - people are interested in hearing your thoughts and opinions on certain topics. Think of that classic ice breaker, "Nice Weather!" and how many times have you just blown it off to start a conversation because what do you have to say about the weather? It's not your fault that the sun isn't out or that the sky isn't blue, I'm just saying that it's not the most interesting thing to everyone else and so they would rather hear about something else.

There are several things that you can do to try and overcome your small talk phobia. The first thing you should do is to try and talk with someone who is similar to you in some way, i.e., an introvert or an extrovert. This will help you get into the flow of small talk without being afraid of being judged for how "unintellectual" or "boring" it seems to be, which is usually what small talk is for introverts anyways.

Once you get into the flow of having small talk with someone, you should try to think of questions that are specific to their field or interest. It's best to ask questions that will require a bit more thought as they will make your conversation more interesting to them and they will want to answer them if you're able to keep a conversation going. For example, rather than saying "Wow! It's hot today!", it would be better to say "I noticed it was unusually warm today when I walked out of work. Is this typical for the end of summer?" They would have much more fun answering this question and so would you since the question requires some thought.

Another way you can overcome small talk is by being more open. There are people out there that would rather have a conversation about their mundane day-to-day life than about some strange topic that's completely unrelated to their life. This can help you get out of your shell a little since people will be more likely to want to talk with you if they feel like you're "just like them".

Third, the most important way to overcome small talk is by being yourself and practicing what I call "human conversation". This means that rather than trying to always have something interesting and unique to say, try and just express yourself. Ironically, the blandest conversations often have the most interesting people in them. There are many things that you can talk about such as your favourite sports, who you think is hot, what do you like to eat, what's your favourite colour, or even your birthday. It's important to avoid talking about yourself as much as possible but if it comes up feel free to talk about yourself. Just be sure not to go on and on or else it will just feel like a big bore, and no one will want to keep up with the conversation. Small talk is a very important way of showing that you're making an effort towards socialising - it shows that you want the other person to connect with you and test the waters of their company before committing more fully.

The key to making small talk

There will be times when you'll interact with complete strangers at a job interview, other guests at a party, or even people you come across in a classroom for a group project. You'll most likely feel very nervous about small talk with these types of people as well (especially if it's just a job interview), but nature has landed you here because we've all been taught since childhood to make small talk.

The best way to break out of your small talk phobia and make small talk with these people is by finding something that you have in common with them. You may have a mutual interest, or they could have made a comment which made you think that they'd be interesting to chat with. If you're at a party, the host will likely be a mutual friend. You could talk of how you met with the host or how you relate. If you're at a class, there may be a professor or two who you can talk about. You could ask them how the work you're doing compares to what he/she does for a living. At the bus station, you could make a comment about the weather or something that an ad poster behind them is advertising. You could talk of how commute times have gotten worse, or how you could save money by buying a car. The examples are endless, just be sure to look around and see if there's anything in the environment that makes you think of something to say first before you try opening your mouth.

You may also want to take a moment to observe the other person as well. If you make eye contact, maintain it for a second or two before looking away (this lets them know that you're interested in them). As an example, once you notice what they're wearing, look at their shoes and again make a comment on theirs. If the person is carrying a purse/bag with them, and its rather unique then ask what brand it is or comment on the style. If others there with them, you can pretend that your question is for everyone and not just for the one person. You can make a comment about how design has changed over the years, or how now men's fashion has evolved beyond the briefcase. It all depends on what you have in common with them, and if they're willing to talk to you then great, they're your new friend.

CHAPTER 2: A MEANINGFUL CONVERSATION

Genuine connections are made, and old relationships are revived when meaningful conversations take place. Meaningful conversations are those that are focused on common interests and needs, and not just general topics such as sports, the weather, or favourite bands. These types of conversations tend to build an emotional bond between the two people involved and they're also more likely to create a closer bond between you and the person whom you're talking with.

An example of a meaningful conversation would be one in where you talk about how getting injured affected you physiologically, or what role it played in your life. You could discuss how you were unable to participate in sports for many years and how it affected your self-esteem, or what your goals were prior to being injured. You could also discuss the psychological effects that pain has on your life due to the intense physical pain that you felt during the time when you injured yourself. The conversation can either be a long one where you talk about things that we've all experienced or a short one if it is something specific to them.

A mundane and meaningless conversation could be about the weather, but this conversation will only serve as a buffer between things that you need to do or something that you want to get out of. It's simply socializing, and it's often what makes up small talk. Meaningful conversations have no rules or expectations for meaning, but there are "topic-guidelines" in which you can follow if you wish. The guidelines are here to help you be more flexible instead of having set limitations on your conversations with others.

A deep conversation with a friend can include things such as one's sexual orientation, their family life and childhood, or a past experience that they kept quiet about for many years. Deep conversations are not only a great way to make friends but are also an excellent way of telling or discovering important information. You may have noticed some people have a very subtle look in their eyes when talking about something that's meaningful to them (like how they're engaged). This look is what sets apart the deep conversations from the bland and meaningless ones.

Going big on the small talk

One mistake we make when conversing is thinking that small talk should just be small talk. It's a way to segue into deeper, more meaningful conversations. We often feel that if we start off with a heavy topic, then it's likely that the conversation will be one-sided and awkward. This isn't the case though because people are much more likely to open up if you start off with something light-hearted. Small talk is a way to break the ice, and by going big on it you're much more likely to have meaningful conversations later on.

You can even use small talk as a tool for making good friends with someone who you have something in common with but aren't sure if they'd like to take the next step. For example, say you've met this really nice person at work and think that they're really interesting. Instead of asking "What's up?" and talking about a random topic, you can say something like "I saw your band play a couple weekends ago and they were amazing. Where did you get your guitar?" You could also talk about that time that you ate at their favourite restaurant and learned how they like to twist their pasta.

After a short talk, you can either ask them if they'd like to go out sometime or if they want to hang out with some of your other friends. By asking this specific type of question, you're encouraging the other person to make the connection between what they've just spoken about (their band) and something in your own life (your favourite food). If you do this correctly, the other person will start to ask, "So what about your favourite food?". This is a great way of starting off a conversation with someone because it shows that you're interested in them and their opinions.

To make small talk more meaningful, you have to start off with something relatable. This can be done by talking about small, simple, everyday things that relate to the person you're talking to. People enjoy learning about other people's lives because it makes them more interested in what they have to say and their opinions. Instead of asking "How was your weekend?", ask "Did you walk?" or "Did you bike?". The other person will respond by saying "Yeah, I biked to the park with my friends." You can then ask them "How long did it take? Was it fun?" or "Did you do anything else?".

By asking meaningful questions, you'll get a more detailed response. This will help you to build a stronger connection with the other person and can make for some great small talk.

Engage in dialogue instead of monologues. Conversations don't have to be about you. You want people to feel comfortable to let their guard down and talk about their lives, so when they do let it slip out something relatable if possible.

Transitioning from small talk

After exchanging pleasantries, knowing when and how to move on to a meaningful conversation is the next step in building rapport. If you've ever tried to discuss more serious matters with someone who is uncomfortable and unresponsive, you may have learned the hard way that it's difficult to pivot from superficial talk to a sincere and meaningful dialogue. There are ways, however, which can make this transition easier, smoother, and more natural.

- Have some deep conversation starters ready

First, have some deep conversation starters ready. Questions like "What is holding you back from actualizing your dreams". This question will show the other person that you are interested in them. This will make them feel special and they will be open to explaining their dreams and passions. The next thing you have to do is reciprocate. Let the other person say what they are passionate about and also what makes them feel fulfilled. You can start talking about some of your passions, but you should not focus all of your attention on yourself. Remember this is a deep conversation starter, so focus on the other person too.

Questions that start with "What do you wish..." many times lead to deep answers and emotions. Questions like "What do you wish you would have known at 20 that you know now?" or "What do you wish our country could be better at?". These types of questions allow the person to think out loud and to say what they really feel. This will make the other person feel more and more comfortable with you. Other deep conversation starters include "What is the number one problem in our culture today?" or "What can we do to help each other become better in life?". These are simple questions, but they make people think. And that's what a deep conversation is all about. You have to let people think and they will be much more excited to talk with you.

- Talk of things that you're passionate about

Enthusiasm is contagious. When you're passionate about something, you are more likely to talk about it and others will feel your enthusiasm. So, when you have topics to discuss that is your strength, make sure to talk about them. For example, if you're a runner, make sure you talk about running and your running experience. If you're a musician, then make sure you talk about music and discuss strategies or the ups and downs of being a musician. Don't just share information but also share stories. This will show people that you are like them, and they may feel more comfortable with talking with you. You can also share your fears, frustrations, or anything else that makes you happy or sad.

Talk about things that make you happy and inspire others to do the same. You have to show people that you are a positive person who has something to give to the world. This is the only way you will get respect from others, and they will treat you as an equal.

- Use leading statements

There are those things that we love talking about: Things like where we see ourselves in the next 5 years, those moments we'd like to relive, our proudest memories, the first thing people notice about us, our biggest fears... To transition from small talk to a deeper conversation you need to appeal to the feel-good hormone of the person you're talking to. Dopamine.

The neurochemicals get released when we feel pleasure, which can trigger a series of impulses that lead to desire and motivation. That's why we always want more, be it food, sex, money, or drugs. We're hardwired to seek pleasure and happiness. That same neurochemical rush is what makes us bond with people. If you don't appeal to the feel good in that moment, you'll inevitably be rejected and feel bad about yourself.

Ask lifting questions like "What's the best experience you've ever had?" or "What are you most proud of?"

You're not asking about their job, their life, random facts about them that doesn't matter to you.

Ask them about things which mean the most to them. Allow them to be vulnerable and open themselves up to bonding with you.

Leading up your questions with a statement makes it a lot easier for someone to answer it. For example:

"I just love seeing people passionate about something they're doing."

"I'm always curious what makes someone feel truly fulfilled."

It feels like you're "baiting" them to open up and feeling another wave of dopamine as they feel that you're genuinely interested in them. (Note: do NOT go for the obvious opening line like "Tell me about yourself" or "What do you do for a living?")

"I'm curious about the people who are most successful..."

"Why do you think some people seem to be so much luckier than others?"

You're literally asking them to share their greatest insight and it's incredibly powerful. People don't mind answering such questions as they want to connect with other people. Telling them how you feel is also a great way to open up and be vulnerable. For example:

"I feel so inspired by you."

"You're so inspiring."

You must appeal to their feel good to make them open up to you. You want the conversation to flow naturally even if it's about finding love, their achievements, their hobbies and causes they care about.

I'm sure a lot of people have experienced similar situations like the ones above, where they can't think of anything interesting or insightful in which to start a conversation with someone they fancy. The best way around this would be to make statements that make them think about how they feel.

You're seeking for stories, not answers. People love talking about their lives and experiences. You have to make them feel like you're interested in what they have to say, not just listening to a monologue of random facts or experiences. Adopt a curiosity mindset.

Remembering names

We've all been with that person who's so fascinating, she makes you feel like the most captivating person in the room. And when it's time to leave and you're exchanging contact info, you can't recall her name. This happens all too often in mixed company that's full of strangers — it can make us look bad. So, how do you remember everyone's name if you don't want people to think that you're an imbecile? The trick is to actively listen. It's not that you suck at remembering names, you're just not focusing on the conversation. When someone says their name and you can't remember it two seconds after, you were inattentive; and that's not a memory thing, it's a concentration issue. The answer: listen and concentrate. If you do it well, you'll be cruising through your next cocktail party.

- Say the name out loud

Say the person's name out loud, when they tell you their name. Let's say that they've told you "Meet, my wife Sarah. She's from New York." You say, "Hi, Sarah. Nice to meet you".

Let's say that you're talking to Josh, who has just told you that he's a computer technician. You remind yourself by saying, "Josh, you seem to be a great computer technician". "Yeah, I am", Josh says. When you say something like this, it makes people feel that you're interested in them. They think "Wow! You get it!" You're not just saying their name for the sake of saying it; you're actually interested in who they are and so are they.

- Think of someone else with the same name

If you've just met Josh, who's a computer technician, and you know another Josh, who works in human resources, try to think of this other Josh when you meet the computer technician. Associate the name "Josh" with someone else that you know who also has that name. You'll be able to remember it better if you think of them as two different people.

- Make a funny association

Who's the most famous Mike you know of? Mickey Mouse? Mike Tyson? Michael Jordan? Whatever you decide, make a funny association with the person's name that will stick in your head. Use this association during the conversation and you'll be able to recall the person's name when it comes time to contact them later. You can do this with any name; just find something funny about it. For example, I'm sure you can think of a way to associate my last name — James — with a character from Queen of the South, or Twilight or the Godfather. These associations will surely help you remember my name. Remember that your associations don't have to make sense to anyone but you. Obviously, it helps if it's a person with the same name as the person who's talking to you.

- Ask again!

You'd probably rather die of embarrassment than ask them again, right? Wrong! If you don't remember their name and you neglect to ask them, they're bound to think that you're a jerk. But if they've just told you their name and you've already forgotten it - they're going to feel bad for your sake! They'll think "Poor guy! His memory is gone!". Once you've asked them again, it will serve as a cue for your memory and the next time that your meet again, which could be the same day, or at some other event in the near future, the name will pop up in your head.

Social situations are amusing, the longer you wait before asking someone to remind you their name, the more awkward it will be when you finally do it.

Reading emotion through facial expressions

Facial expressions are very powerful in conversation. They can literally tell volumes about the person who's talking to you. If you're not a good reader of them, you may be missing an opportunity for a connection. Unfortunately, most people don't pay attention to facial expressions and so they see the world through their own eyes and filter everything that happens around them from their own point of view.

If you're not good at telling how the person's feeling, you can miss out on connecting emotionally. For example, if you ask a person how he is and he tells you that he's fine, when he clearly looks upset, this means that not only are you not able to read facial expressions but also that you don't understand the difference between being "fine" and being calm. Most people would agree that "fine" is a general term which can be used in different situations. It can mean:

- I'm doing great!

- I'm alright…

- I feel pretty good…

"Fine", in the sense of feeling good isn't the same as when someone says they feel great. When they say "fine", they want you to focus on their happiness and not the situation that they face. If someone tells you that they're fine, but their body language says otherwise, ask them if there's something going on. If it's something simple (like an annoying co-worker), it would be okay to say "No, I don't think it's something bad. I was just wondering if all is well." but this doesn't mean you have to ask them again if everything is alright every time you talk to them. You need to be a good listener and let your host express what he needs from the conversation.

Changes in facial expressions When someone is emotionally stirred, their facial expressions change. If you're looking for a sign that something's going on in their life, you'll have to observe these changes.

- Their eyes widen or narrow

- Their eyebrows raise or lower

- Their lips curl up or down

- They move closer to you or away from you

If someone's eyebrows are raised extremely high, arching over the top of their forehead (known as "nervous" eyebrow raise), then understand that they're feeling uneasy about something. If you've just made a remark that you think might be offensive, then this would be a good time to apologize or change the subject. If someone's lips are curled up and they're looking at you with disgust or anger, it's probably best that you leave the conversation.

Sending the right message

We use our bodies to communicate with others. When meeting new people, gestures and postures can have a strong influence on how others perceive us. In fact, the nonverbal cues you send can be so powerful that they can even backfire, making you seem too strong or shy. Here are a few body-language hacks to try on your next meet and greet.

1. Keep your hands loose while holding a drink

This is one of the best ways to show that you're comfortable in an event and welcome new interactions. Hands clasped around a drink — or worse, around other people — may give off an overly-formal vibe that makes people feel uncomfortable approaching you. A "drink shield" is when you hold a drink close to your chest, as if you're hiding behind it.

2. Use your hands to direct the conversation

When meeting new people, you can use your hands to direct the conversation towards pleasant topics. When talking about an event, use your palms to show you want to talk about it. You can also "cross fingers" or point at things or people.

3. Mirror body language, but do it subtly

Mirroring someone's body language shows that you're listening and interested without the need to ask questions. Similar to the previous point, use your palms when talking about yourself or an event, or keep your arms low in a relaxed way.

4. Get close, but not too close

Many people think they should stand closer to others when meeting new people, but this isn't always the case. Standing too far away can make you seem aloof and uninterested in conversation — this creates awkward moments of silence when someone attempts to talk with you, and you have to subtly move closer."

You can lean in when a person says something you find interesting, but not too much. Leaning in over an object, such as food or drink, can be interpreted as unwanted flirting.

5. Avoid fidgeting

Today's social settings may be a bit more relaxed than in the past, but fidgeting is still a bad idea — particularly when meeting new people. Whether you're playing with your hair, straightening your clothes, or playing with objects on the table, there's nothing subtle about it. Fidgeting can also signal boredom or nervousness.

Chapter 3: Wit and Charm

If you've watched Seinfeld, you know that verbal wittiness is a crucial skill. On the show, Jerry Seinfeld (played by Jerry Seinfeld) is renowned for his ability to make people laugh effortlessly at just about anything. A quick glance at his IMDb profile will show he's also considered one of the best stand-up comedians in the world.

Wit is an elusive skill. It's like verbal charm and it can be learned through observation and practice just like any other skill. It's not about repeating memorized jokes. It's about finding something unique to say to a stranger in a way that makes them laugh naturally.

So, if you're in a place where you have to talk to new people (like at a job interview, or at a speed dating event, or at a networking event) this chapter is on how to be witty and charming when talking to new people.

Seinfeld is able to make people laugh because he's genuinely interested in them as people. He goes out of his way to understand his audience, so that he can find some common ground with them. When you're able to find a similarity between yourself and a stranger, both of you will feel more comfortable around each other. That feeling of comfort leads to good conversations which makes people feel like they've known each other for a long time even though they just met minutes ago.

This is why many friends share the same interests, hobbies, and even quirks.

It becomes easier to talk to strangers when:

- You are genuinely interested in their life.

- You understand their interests.

- You have at least some things in common with your conversation partner.

So, if you want to be witty and charming when talking to people, you need to be interested in them as people, and not just as a means of giving them the answer they want. You'll find that being witty is a natural consequence of talking about what really interests them — like job opportunities or relationship advice — instead of just repeating memorized one-liners from your favourite sitcoms.

While wit uses humour to make people laugh, charm uses attractiveness to make people want to be around you. The two are closely related — attraction leads to wit — and both use words, but charm is more about body language and tone of voice.

One of the biggest mistakes people make when talking to new people is jumping from topic to topic without paying close attention to the other person's interests. They focus on selling themselves instead of listening closely and finding things they have in common with their conversation partner.

Listening

How do you find out common topics of conversation with new people? Through active listening. Active listening is the act of nodding along, smiling, and repeating what you heard without interrupting. It's about being a good listener so that you can see what else the listener has to say. It's also about trying to connect with your conversation partner by asking insightful questions that resonate with their experiences. To become an active listener, you need to show that you're listening.

How do you show that you're listening? Nodding. Smiling. Repeating. These simple gestures will make your conversation partner feel like you're actually interested in their life, instead of just trying to sell yourself to them. If they mention something they're excited about, nod your head and say, "That sounds really exciting" or say "I can't wait to see the finished product." If they mention something they're struggling with, nod your head and say "I understand what you mean. I've had that same problem in the past."

The mirroring technique is where you repeat back what your conversation partner said. This is easiest when they've just finished talking and you want to clarify something they said that you didn't understand or didn't agree with. If they mention a funny experience, mirroring their expression shows that you're listening and interested in what they're saying. Of course, this technique is about mirroring body language, not exactly repeating the exact words that were said.

Do not interrupt them while they're speaking. Do not change the subject while they're speaking. Instead, wait until they finish and say "That's really interesting. I'd love to hear more about that." If your conversation partner is talking to you, don't just respond with memorized one-liners (like an actor in a play). Instead, actively listen and add value to their conversation by asking insightful questions that resonate with their experiences.

Asking the good questions

Questions are a good way to gauge whether you can connect with a new person or not. If you always make the exact same job-related questions, they may seem like they have no value — but when asked with good intention, they have the power to evoke an authentic feeling of connection in people.

Asking good questions shows you're interested in what they have to say, and it allows them to open up to you. Good questions aren't just about asking who, what, when and where — they're also about showing that you understand their situation and how they feel about it. If they tell you something that's difficult for them, rather than asking them what happened or how it went, ask "How did that make you feel?" or "What do you think about this situation?"

Let's say that you're having a conversation with someone, and they mention a very exciting experience where they took a trip to a foreign country. Here are some examples of the types of questions you can ask:

- "Tell me more about that trip." This shows that you're actively interested in what they're saying. It also gives you an opportunity to find out more about their experience. This is a good question. We could make it better by narrowing it down to specific parts of their trip — like the sights, or the weather, or the culture. Instead of asking "Tell me more about that experience" it'd be better to ask "What did you think of the food in Florida. Do they eat differently from the way we do in the north?" By asking questions that show you're actively listening, you'll find other things you have in common with them. This is a good way to see if we can connect on a deeper level than just friendly banter.

- "What was that experience like?" or "What made that experience so special to you?" This shows that you listened and understood what they were saying. It's a great question because it's specific and shows you think about their experiences. Also, by asking it, you're adding value to the conversation. You're not just asking this because it's on your mind — instead, you're genuinely interested in what they have to say about their experience. They'll likely comment on how it was the most beautiful place they've ever seen, and you can ask follow-up questions to find out why that's important to them.

Adding in your experiences

This is not just about asking questions. You need to add value to their experience by showing that you've had similar situations in the past or that you understand what they're talking about. For example, "I used to live in San Diego for a short period of time and I remember the weather was hot and dreary when I moved there from Arizona. I know exactly how you feel."

Asking too many questions turns a conversation into an interview. You need to show that you're listening. But don't just do this by asking relevant questions. Interact with your conversation partner and find out what else they have in common with you. And if you've never had the same experience, don't lie about it — instead, ask them to tell you more about their experience and why it's important to them.

As they're speaking, find things that you can talk about with them. If they mention something that you've dealt with before, share your experience. Let's say that you're speaking to someone who's going through a difficult time at work, they've told you about that micromanaging boss they have. If you've dealt with the same thing, don't just ask them how they're handling their situation. Tell them how you handled it and how it worked out in the end.

You could say "I know exactly how that feels. For me, it was when I moved from Toronto to San Diego. I was working as a graphic designer, and I had to report to my boss every day. It was an insane amount of pressure for me because he would give me constant criticism when I didn't do things the way he wanted them done. I ended up quitting because I couldn't stand it anymore, but it made me realize that you have to follow your own path in life."

Showing that you're empathetic is important, but don't just do this with your words, you need to show empathy through your body language. This means looking at them and nodding while they're talking — this shows that you're engaged in their conversation. If they've mentioned something that you can talk about, don't just jump in — give them a moment to get the words out. Don't cut them off or interrupt them. Also, avoid doing things like checking your phone or hunching over in your chair as it shows that you're not interested in what they're saying.

Developing genuine curiosity

When you're genuinely interested in someone and you want to know more about them, they'll notice this. It makes a huge difference if you're genuinely curious about what they have to say — rather than just being polite by asking whatever comes to mind. It helps if you can direct the conversation to topics that you have in common — things that you can talk about that show that you're listening. For example, if they're talking about their family, you might say "My sister's living in Los Angeles now and she moved with her family from Canada to San Diego. I'm excited to meet her for the first time. What made you choose to move there?"

By taking an interest in what they're saying, you're showing that you value them and their time. You're not just doing this because you want something from them — instead, you want to get to know them and have a conversation that's exciting and meaningful to both of you. If they see that they can trust you and open up to you, they'll enjoy the conversation and look forward to talking again.

Recognizing conversational styles

Different people like to communicate in different ways. The style of communication that's most comfortable for you won't necessarily be the same as the one that's most comfortable for someone else. If you're having a conversation with someone who prefers a different style of communication, it can be easy to misinterpret their message and react negatively. If you recognize their preferred style, however, it will be much easier for you to stay on the same page as them and not get frustrated or angry by miscommunication. In this section, you'll learn to understand the different types of communication styles and how you can interact with people of different types.

- Assertive communication style

An assertive person is prepared to express their ideas and opinions, even if they're not always right. If a conversation doesn't go their way, they're willing to be honest about what they want and where they're at — while being able to compromise themselves. Their confidence in themselves and the way that they present themselves makes it much easier for them to be understood by others. Assertiveness is part of their personality.

When you're conversing with someone who's assertive, you can use interruptions to ask them questions about themselves and what they're doing. They're usually very honest and open about their lives, so you don't have to worry about them being evasive. They're usually interested in what you've got to say, too.

They tend to have strong opinions about things but are open to hearing your point of view. This is a good way for you to show that you're interested in having a meaningful conversation.

- Aggressive communication style

When you're talking with someone who's aggressive, it can be difficult to know whether they're being sincere or just trying to manipulate you through sarcasm or aggression. They don't usually mean to behave this way, but they may sometimes act in an abrasive way because they feel their ideas and opinions aren't being taken seriously. It can be hard for them to express their ideas without coming across as aggressive because they want people to listen. They're usually polite and open, but they speak a lot because they prefer to catch their listener's attention rather than waiting for them to pay attention.

Pay attention to the facial expressions and body language of the people you're speaking with if they're aggressive. This can help you to understand how they're feeling and what they mean by what they say to you.

Aggressive people are often really good at talking in a convincing way. They can be really interesting to talk with because of their passion, but it's so important that you don't feel disrespected by their tone or by any manipulation their using. You should also try not to interrupt or challenge them unless you have an assertive personality yourself — otherwise, it's very likely that they'll use aggressive manipulation to come across as the person in charge of the conversation.

- Passive communication style

When you start talking with someone who's a passive speaker, it can be difficult for them to express themselves fully. They're not usually in control of the direction of the conversation. They may keep changing their mind about what they want to talk about because they've got lots of things that they want to say and an enormous amount of information that they want to share. Although they're very polite and considerate, they'll change the topic of conversation so much that it won't always seem clear what they want to talk about. They're more comfortable telling you about a variety of things rather than being more direct.

Passive people are usually very polite in the way that they speak — both in terms of their word choice and the tone of their voice — but it can sometimes be difficult to know whether or not you've offended them. This can present you with a challenge because, although it may seem like passive people don't really care whether or not they offend you, they actually do care tremendously.

It can be difficult for passive people to give you their complete attention because of the way that they talk. If you ask them a question or comment on something that they've said, they'll probably ask you to elaborate or repeat it — which can make it seem like they're not really listening.

Passive communicators are thought to be "boring" because they don't use a lot of dramatic or exaggerated language. They actually prefer to use a lot of adjectives and adverbs.

People who are agreeable speak in a very friendly way. They want to be liked by everyone, which can sometimes make it challenging for them to share their opinions and draw any kind of conclusion from the conversation. They'll tend to smile, laugh and be really positive in the way that they speak so that people will like them, but they may also agree with the opinions of other people without offering up many suggestions or ideas themselves.

They're usually very nice people and you can count on them to be kind and supportive of you.

- Manipulative communication style

People who speak in a manipulative way usually aren't used to hearing the things other people have to say. This means that they may interrupt them and challenge them directly. They like to be the centre of attention and want people to listen when they're talking — which can be challenging for you if you don't like being interrupted or told what to do.

If you start talking with someone who's manipulative, it's important that you don't let your frustration get the best of you. Instead, it would be a good idea to just listen to what they have to say and take it into consideration. They're usually very excited and passionate about the things they have to say, but there may also be a lot of emotion in the way that they speak.

Manipulators tend to use exaggerated language in order to prove their point, so you shouldn't worry about them being seen as boring because of this. They would probably rather tell you their opinions than let you make your own conclusions about things anyway!

Matching their style

Any type of communicator can learn to listen better, but people who speak in an aggressive way may need to practice the most. It's not easy for them to listen when they feel like they're at the center of attention.

Agreeable people really enjoy listening to other people, so if you have a disagreement with someone who speaks in a manipulative or passive way, they're usually very good at calming them down and helping them understand where you're coming from.

Passive communicators are actually very good listeners — although their tendency is to change the subject rather than being open about what they want to talk about.

Everyone has their own unique way of speaking, so don't worry if you've never spoken to someone who uses passive or aggressive communication before. It doesn't mean that it's not worth trying to communicate with them, or that you should assume that they're no different from anyone else when it comes to learning how to communicate better.

Know your personal triggers. If you tend to be passive or aggressive yourself, it might take a bit more effort for you to learn how to better listen. Learn the language of your own personality and be aware of what words and phrases make you feel frustrated or upset.

Don't make assumptions about what someone else's personality is like. Even if they're a passive speaker, it doesn't mean that they don't have any personality at all. It's good to keep an open mind and be willing to try out new strategies.

Instead of being hard on yourself, use your understanding of your own feelings and communication style as a motivation for learning how to listen better. If you've always been passive in conversation, it might be difficult for you to listen when someone uses more aggressive communication techniques. For example, if someone has really strong opinions or is challenging you directly, you might have trouble controlling yourself enough to pay attention quietly while they're talking.

Somewhat vulnerable

Exposing your vulnerabilities brings out the humanness in you, which can make the other person feel bonded to you. People like to feel close to each other, and vulnerability helps with this.

Your emotions and feelings are the deepest part of you and having them exposed brings up a sensitive and gentle side that shows how vulnerable you are. This is not a weakness on your part. It's an act of trusting the other person enough to be vulnerable with them, which they will appreciate because they may also be vulnerable with you at times.

Let's say that you're talking about something that's really close to your heart. You're sharing your innermost feelings and emotions, and you might feel like you're putting yourself in a vulnerable position. At the same time, you may also realise that simply by expressing yourself in this way, it brings out the best in you — and it might also bring out the best in the other person. If you were speaking of a time when you were laid off, you could say something like "I was really upset and scared, but when I realised that I could get out of that situation, another possibility opened up for me."

If the person you were taking to has shared an embarrassing experience with you, he or she will probably have a more open attitude toward you and feel that you're someone who's like them. It's about letting your guard down and having the person feel like they can be themselves with you.

When you say things like "I never had the courage to talk to people like I do with you" or "No one really knows me as well as you do," the other person will feel flattered, and they'll be more willing to give their own vulnerabilities to you.

Chapter conclusion: An exercise on rambling

In this chapter, we've seen how wit and charm help in communication. But what can you do if you're struggling to find something to talk about? Ramble. Rambling is the art of having long-winded conversations stemming from trivial topics, i.e., making small talk. This exercise will help you learn how to make conversations flow like the river, making them seem more interesting and relaxed.

Step 1: Choose an object that's near you. It could be a plant, a flower nearby, a sign on the wall or a piece of paper on your table. It could even be something intangible; like an ice cream flavour.

Step 2: Once you have your object, ask yourself what to talk about with that in mind. You might start by saying something like

- "I wonder how ice cream goes through its production process. I mean, how can they blend that many flavours together? Are those workers trained professionals of some sort?"

- "Servers at restaurants have to be really patient, I think. The experiences they went through could make good stories."

- "There's a really pretty flower over there in the courtyard, right? I don't know what kind it is, but it's gorgeous!"

- "Netflix is a nice service. But the fact that we get to choose the exact show we want, or the movie of our preference, is amazing! It's like we're having a personal orchestra playing for us!"

- "Sometimes I wonder how students who don't have a lot of money get their books at school. I mean, I know there are book fairs and stuff, but not always can you get what you want from those."

- "The world is changing around us so fast. You think about how many years it took for trains to become common in some countries. Or look at what's happening with self-driving cars right now."

Step 3: Think of the "ideal" attribute that this object should have.

If the object you chose is a chair, you might say something like.

-"Orange isn't a great colour for a chair at least in this space with the current interior design. I think black is better."

- "I don't think this chair was made for our body type. It feels like it's for a child or someone with a long torso."

- "Smartphones can now record videos in slow motion. That's really cool, but I wonder how many people still need that kind of quality."

- "I feel like this bus is going too fast. Maybe that's because I haven't slept properly."

Step 4: Make funny or weird comments about the object you chose:

- "This book is huge. It makes me feel like a child when I hold it"

- "I wonder what's the worst thing that has happened to these pages of my book? It feels like someone spilled coffee all over them."

- "This book is really old. It would be interesting to find out who wrote it and what he's working on at the moment."

Step 5: Describe the memories that the object sparks

-"Growing up, I remember my parents telling me that books are for looking up and not for playing with. I'm glad to learn that this book has actually been played with a lot, because it would be boring if it sat in a bookcase like it's an old relic."

- "This book is really old. I wonder how much time it took to write it and why it was written. It must have been really fascinating in its day."

- "A lot of people like to tell a story at the beginning of their novels but then they just write a bunch of boring events without giving us a point or any meaning behind them."

- "When I was living in Korea, I remember that in some schools they made us take an English class. We were expected to learn English by reading a lot of books and having classes, but most of the time we just read in the classroom."

Whenever you run out of things to talk about during a conversation, you can always fall back on objects, their attributes, and the memories they evoke. Let's put this into perspective. You're having lunch with a potential client for your new business. You want to establish a good relationship with him so that he'll work with you. You're thinking of things to talk about, but nothing seems relevant. Then you remember that he had said at the beginning of the meeting that he has recently returned from vacation in Greece after visiting the Parthenon.

This instantly makes you think of that beautiful white structure and the many wonderful memories of your own experiences at European museums. You're then reminded of your last trip to Paris where you were close to going inside the Louvre where some of the most famous works in the world are held. You think about how awesome it is to see this stuff up close and how you were able to visit so many museums during your stay. You then tell him all about your trips, how fun they were, what you saw and what you learned from them. The key here is to not just start talking randomly but rather choosing a random object that sparks off a context for a more interesting conversation.

Even a TV show can serve as a base of a conversation. If you're talking about *Stranger Things* for example, you can start telling people about the mullet hairstyle that the character Joyce has and how it reminds you of your childhood, at which point you proceed to tell them about things that happened to you while living in a small town.

Key takeaway

Whenever you find yourself struggling to remember what to talk about, you can always fall back on objects, their attributes, and the memories they evoke. Imagine that you're sitting in a room with a new acquaintance and neither of you really knows the other. You could start by talking about the room itself or anything in it. Ideally, if someone were to hear this conversation for example, he would've have heard the most boring conversation in the history of mankind. But it's not about sounding interesting to others. It's about being interesting to each other and sparking a bit of a connection between two people who are meeting for the first time. So instead of saying something like "This leather sofa is nice", you could say something like "This leather sofa is very comfortable, but it also has so many scratches and scars on it that I wonder how long it takes for this type of a leather to fade".

Instead of saying "It's a little bit boring when people just tell you what they're going to do next week", you could say "I'm really curious about the life of people with very busy schedules, how their days go and what they get up to when they're not working. It must be a big relief when your life is planned out for you, so everything is in the right place, and you don't have to worry about anything".

Instead of saying "This man is dressed very nicely." you could say "I'm so scared of speaking to someone in a fancy suit because I think I might do something wrong like spill my drink on his shoes or pick up the wrong fork and drop it on his table. But then again, it's a little bit silly to talk too much about clothes. There's no shame if you don't have the money to have a beautiful suit but you've still got a lot of other things that count".

Instead of saying "This book is really old. I wonder how much time it took to write it and why it was written", you could say "Even though this book has been used so many times, the cover still looks sturdy. I wonder how these covers are made and what kind of material they use. Does something look wrong with the spine? Maybe someone should re-stretch the cover, so the paper doesn't get yellow and worn at the edges".

These are only simple examples but do you see the pattern?

CHAPTER 4: THE ARE METHOD

Carol A. Fleming, a communication coach who's been in the business for forty years came up with a "fool-proof" method for initiating small talk. She calls it the Anchor, Reveal, Encourage method. In a nutshell, you'll be looking for a common topic to talk about (the anchor), revealing a little bit of information about yourself, and then encourage the other person to do the same.

You need to be careful though. Since we've learned that small talk is really about establishing rapport and connection with another human being, you won't want to reveal everything about yourself in just a few sentences. It's more about revealing one little thing that will elicit positive feelings from the other person and make them want to continue talking to you. Let's look at the ARE method in detail.

The anchor

This is what connects you and the person you want to make small talk with. If you're at the subway waiting for a train, it could be the train, public transit, or even the city itself. In college, it could be common classes, the same dorm, a recent exam, or sports teams. In a social gathering, it could be the weekend, mutual friends, a popular TV show, or food.

Not everyone has to be interested in the same topic. In fact, it's very likely that there will be a lot of differences between you and the person you want to talk with. But that doesn't mean you can't find common ground. If this person is sharing an interest of yours, it's much easier to connect with them than if they were completely random.

To initiate the conversation, use an opening line that features the anchor. I'll use examples to illustrate this

- "Hey, you're in my math class."

- "Oh hey, aren't we in the same area?" (referring to university or dorm zone)

- "Wow, you look so familiar but I can't place where I know you from."

- "Did you like that sandwich? I've been meaning to ask you about it" (referring to an interesting food at the party)

Reveal

This is where you reveal a little bit of information about yourself. Remember not to give out too much information. Like I mentioned before, it's more about establishing a connection and building rapport. Your goal here is to make them feel like they have something in common with you so they feel compelled to continue talking with you.

The Reveal

This is where you make a personal remark that builds up on the anchor you've just used. It could be an interesting fact, a new hobby, or a personal experience. It could also be something that you have that's similar to the object of the conversation. For example, if you're talking about travel, you could mention something about your travel plans that connect with the conversation. If it's about art, you could talk about some piece of art that you like (even if it isn't related to the conversation at hand). Here are a few examples.

- "When I was in Spain I visited the Monasterio de Santo Domingo. It was amazing!"

- "I love interior design and by the way, this door knob reminds me of my grandma's house."

- "I just read this interesting article about health trends. Did you know that the more you exercise, the hungrier you get?"

- "I'm really into yoga lately. Do you do any sports?"

The Encouragement

After you've come up with an anchor and added your personal experience it's time to ask a question that encourages the listener to share more. Since you want to keep the conversation going, a simple question will do. Here are examples.

- "What's the funniest health trend you've heard about lately?"

- "That's really interesting. Were you born in the Philippines?"

- "I can't believe that you got to see the same thing I did!"

- "Did you get to see an art museum during your vacation?"

Building the conversation after the ARE

Once a person has answered your question, you'll want to relate their answer back to the topic of conversation. You can also ask them more questions about what they said or ask for their opinion on something relevant to what they said. So, if they said that their favourite colour was blue, you could say" "me too! Blue is my favourite colour too!". If they said that they like dogs, then it would be a good time to ask them what kind of dog they have - or why they think dogs are great companions etc...

Conversations that start with the ARE are meant to be kept light and fun. Invite the other person to talk about something, but don't interrupt them when they're talking. If someone seems monotone or boring, try to change the topic or ask more questions of them. Also, be friendly and charming in your approach.

CHAPTER 5: WHAT IF?

In this chapter, we'll be looking at some of the "challenges" that you might find yourself having when trying to start conversations with new people. I'll be giving you some tips and tricks that might help you overcome them.

First, let's get a few things out of the way.

1. In order for a conversation to be successful, both people need to want to talk. If one person doesn't want to talk then there's nothing in this world that will make them do it.

2. You can rarely predict exactly how conversations will go. Be open minded to the flow of the conversation and be prepared to adjust accordingly.

3. If a conversation can't move forward no matter what you do, then it probably shouldn't be done. It will not help your goal of becoming more socially competent to sit at a party for an hour talking to someone who isn't interested in you.

Let's get to the issues you'll face and how you'll get around them

The conversation keeps stalling

At times, the conversation will come to a natural pause. Use this moment to gauge the person you're talking to's interest. If they try to come up with something else to talk about, then continue with the topic at hand. If they don't try to come up with anything, then this could be a sign that the person isn't invested in the chat as you are. In this case, the best thing to do would be to move on.

If you've run out of stuff to say, ramble about something that's related to what you were talking about earlier. Let's say that you were talking about how you love to travel but have never been overseas. You could start rambling on about the places you've been to in your country. Or if you and the person you're talking to just finished talking about their last job, you can talk about a job that's related to your own.

Hobbies make a great thing to talk about. A lot of people like the same types of activities that you do. Try talking about your favourite books, tv shows, sports or music.

You'll need to change the topic often when it comes to small talk with large groups of people. If you notice that the conversation has died down, try coming up with a new question that's tied to the mutual object/event we talked about in the previous chapter. Something like

- "So, what do you think of this party? It seems like everyone is having a lot of fun."

- "What do you think about video games? Do you play them or watch them?"

- "How does this class compare to yesterday's class?"

It can be hard for the conversation to move forward in certain situations. For example, if there's a group of people talking, you might find it hard to get a word in with everyone talking at once. If you've already tried asking questions and they're not giving you anything, then it's time to end the chat. Thank them for their time and move on.

How do I transition to another subject after exhausting the current topic?

Segueing is a word that's used quite often when talking about conversation. It refers to the way you move from one subject to the next.

How do you segue effectively? Well, let's think about a few examples.

In the movie "The Hangover," when the guys wake up after a night of partying, they have to have some fun with each other to get over their hangovers. They start asking each other questions about their hangovers and reminisce about their night together.

A segue can be as simple as asking someone if they're ready for the next event in your life. Or you could segue with something funny that's happened to you that morning. As long as you can find a way to link what you want to talk about with the current topic, it will work just fine. Let's say that you're talking about pets, and you want to talk about your hometown or a place you've been to. You could make an observation linking the current topic to your hometown. Something like:

- "There aren't many dog breeders where I'm from. When you need a dog, you can just go to the pound and adopt one."

- "Where I'm from, many cats live inside. The streets are too dangerous for them."

- "I'm from a small town, so I don't have shelters around here."

- "When I was in Europe, there were no dogs in the streets. Everyone got their animals from a shelter."

Have you seen how we're 'baiting' the other person to inquire on our hometown or the exact country I visited? There's a chance that they'll bite, and the conversation will flow smoothly!

If you want to start talking about a person's interests, you should make an observation about them. Tell them something about their appearance or what they're wearing that relates to the topic of your conversation. Something like:

- "I love your shirt/hat. Do you have a theme for today?" - If she's wearing a shirt with cats on it, then she may be a cat lover and might have some fun stories to tell you.

- "You have some really nice shoes. Are they comfortable?" The person might reveal where the shoes are from or why they chose them (e.g., comfort)

- "You look like someone who has great taste in music."

- "That necklace you're wearing is beautiful."

- "You have a really unique hairstyle. How long does it typically take to style it like that?"

- "Your tattoo reminds me of a movie character I used to watch. Let me try and find it on Google?"

- "Your glasses make you look mysterious."

Of course, there's a chance that the person won't follow your segue. If they ask you a counter question, flow with it instead. Don't force things.

How do I end a conversation when the person won't stop talking?

At times, you'll meet a chatterbox who'll hold you hostage in a conversation. To get out of the conversation, casually mention that you're running late for an appointment, that you have a family emergency to attend to or that you're feeling ill. Then use the excuse of saying goodbye.

This tactic works best if you've been keeping your end of the conversation. If your counterpart has been dominating the conversation from start to finish, then it's time to stop talking and look for an escape route.

Conclusion

In this book we've seen how we can have meaningful conversations with anyone. We've seen that we can use the ARE method to avoid dead-ends and how to analyse people's appearances to find things that we have in common.

If you really want to master the art of conversation, then you need to practice. Start small by talking with those who are easy to talk with and build up from there. Don't worry if you mess up the first couple of times; we all had a period when we were awkward at making conversation.

PRO TIP: People in retail - cashiers, baristas, waiters, etc. can be a great first group of people to start practicing on. These people are naturally chatty, and you'll learn a lot about their personality and the things going on its way. When you're ordering food at a restaurant, you might ask them how they like living in the city or if they're from here.

The two people at the checkout counter of my local grocery store still remember my family. I've been coming here for ten years, and we always talk about the Halloween decorations, Thanksgiving dinner and when the kids are going to hit the Christmas season. We have fun conversations where I'm making them laugh or learning about things that are going on in their lives. They know what to expect from me because I'm not trying to sell them anything or get anything out of them - it's just a casual conversation about current events and topics that interest us both.

Don't forget that successful conversations aren't just about what you say; they're about how you say it too.

www.ingramcontent.com/pod-product-compliance
Lightning Source LLC
Chambersburg PA
CBHW072107110526
44590CB00018B/3351